2014

How to Succeed in the Job market!

Ways to succeed in your job market and career planning!!!!!!

Jay Kay
Author of '7 Golden Rules of ZEN Wisdom'

ISBN 9781502703866
Published by
Jay Kay
writerjaykay@gmail.com

My deepest pranams to my beloved Guru...

To my family, friends & publishers with gratitute...

Thank you for all your patience and guidance...

Prologue...7
Job Interview 11
Social Media Profile...13
Candidate Selection Criteria 15
Job Interview Process...25
Building A Winning Profile 36
Institute / University...37
Awards / Recognition 38
Organization 38
      Client...**38**

Career Progression 44
Competency Pyramid 45
Types of Organization 51
Five steps for managing client expectations 73
Job Failure – A stepping stone for Success!.................76
Epilogue 79

Success!!!

Success is a choice,

If you think,

You believe,

You will

Succeed…

The belief is within you,

And the success is just a mile away!

You can do it,

With persistence behavior!

Success is a choice,

If you believe in yourself,

You will succeed!

- Jay Kay

*

Dedication

To all my bosses, leaders, colleagues & interviewers
those who have intimidated me through my
professional career.

Thank you for helping me progress in my career!

Prologue

Success is the mantra of the yester years. None of you like failures isn't? How would you enjoy success in your endeavors without knowing the pains of a failure?

As a matter of fact, every successful person has gone through tremendous confronting situations, the ultimate testimony of their characters. If you are able to exercise your "Will" power during tough times, the pleasant times will arrive. After all, success is just the other side of a failure.

Have you realized this phenomenon? When you look at your failures and contemplate on it..You had learnt someone beyond, very uplifting in your life. It is your life time endeavor and there is no need to hanker on success alone.

If you fail, just accept it. You've been conditioned to race for success in the market place..and the real connotation of success is the quality of life that you lead in terms of physical, mental and spiritual well being in your life. How many of you had an opportunity to reflect on the term "success"

What does success mean to you?

In your life and professional career! Ofcourse, monetary gains are part of a successful professional career, truth is that there is no success on the day when you're promoted at work and filed for divorse at home. It has to be balanced. Success is the physical, mental and spirital well-being that each of you want to achieve sub-consciously, however you get diverted in the journey, thereby missing the broader perspectives in life.

If you chase money alone, you'd fail, instead if you plan for a career that you're passionate about, you would suceed, and money is just the byproduct of a successful career. It doesn't matter how much money you have..how much you're living in the present moments is what ultimately counts. There is no point is spending money at a hospital..hence, it is a social responsibility to maintain a physical, mental & emotional well-being before you progress to the ultimate spiritual progression.

We all work to suceed and nobody wants to fail. How would you achieve success if your actions are not aligned to the laws of Universe. If your actions are done correcly, the results would be right. It is your intepretation of success or failure. Nature is a Divine Justice, where the results will be in accord with the cause and effect system. What you do is what you would reap up!

If you are really striving hard to achieve success in your personal and a professional career, here is an opportunity to understand the broader views to succeed by taking a step towards planning your career and take necessary corrective actions to succeed in your life.

A real successful person is the one, who is able to comprehend the truths by attunment of mind to the Universe and who lives his life joyously in unison with Nature. Ofcourse monetary funds have to be used diligently to achive this ultimate feat of succes, not to get entagled with the money alone. It has to be used for achieving broader vision in life. You cannot medidate if your basic needs aren't fulfilled. You should strive hard to fulfill your basic needs and maintain enough to sustain yourself through the life term to be able to spend on high quality things in life to be able to pursue your passion. For example. My passion is writing books, poetry and learning music, I cannot pursue my dreams, unless and until my basic needs are fulfilled.

A real knowledge is the ability to turn-in and view things with a different perspective. There is no need to study metaphysics in the University, perhaps you can observe it within yourself and the surroundings to achieve a different quality of life.

Life has many problems with more confronting situations at work, society, politics and relationships etc. You cannot seek a life without problems. It depends on how you manage them, by turning your challenges to a success. Each of these events will teach you something.

Often most of you fail in your endeavors due to lack of planning and due-diligence in life. If you're able to transform your failures to learnings and move on, then you will be able to achieve your feat of success. Mostly you fail in your endeavors due to lack of risk taking apetite, you're stuck into an endeavor without much progress. It is required to plan your career and progress to build the right expertise in a sustainable career.

This book is an invitation to all of you working towards a common goal of achieving success in life. As the first step, this book will guide you towards a successful job interview and career planning & progression.

Job Interview

T he first step before you attend
any interview is to understand the process. There are
multiple teams involved in shortlisting your profile
for an interview, based on skills, selection process
and the internal/external teams involved in the
recruitment process. There are specialized skill based
agencies known as recruitment firms specialized in
recruitment. In most of the cases the Talent
Acquisition group (TAG) is entirely responsible for
recruitment, building competencies & nuture talent
for the Organization. In summary, an Organization is
looking forward to engaging the right skills set for
the successful delivery of the project.

In a typical IT environment, you will need to
register your profile in a job portal such as
Naukri.com, Jobsahead.com, Monster.com,

HeadHonchos.com or use your mobile app to register. Once you register your details, your profile will be reviewed by potential employers, and agencies.

The following process map will help you understand the details of the interview process:

The above work flow indicates sequence of tasks performed as part of the recruitment process. The Talent Acquisition Group (TAG) is responsible for recruiting the right hire. They may employ an agency as a partner, who are specialized in identifying the talent. They will register in a job portal with clear Job description on the behalf of the client.

Once they short list candidates based on fitment of a profile, TAG will send a profile to the IT dept for technical scrutiny. If a candidate passes through the criteria for selection, it goes for another round of management discussions and finally to the HR for evaluating the overall credentials, behavior and past job history. Finally, they review your profile with the market trend for the position and align you to a specific salary and discuss benefits in the final round.

Social Media Profile

Your profile should be created in the social media to enhance your chances of finding the right Organization. It is a good practice to maintain up-to-date profile in every months to ensure you're ahead of the market, even if you're not searching. Keep your research about the Industry segment, market atleast every six months. This step would help you in case of any unexpected layoff's. I have observed many TAG teams of reputed MNC's fishing out the best candidates through the social media network such as linkedin network, facebook etc.

You should maintain your profile in the social media network and in addition build your podcasts, project artifacts and store it in the cloud space to ensure availability during the interview process. You can just pass on the links to ensure the interviewer reviews each of these specifics. Perhaps you can take snaps of your project awards, celebrations video and post it in your video profile to justify significant accomplishments. A simple 2 mins video should portray about yourself. Your accomplishments and projects, technology, business process expertise to create a **wow** factor in your interviewer even before he meets you face-to-face. I would recommend investing in a simple portal describing about yourself, links about the projects, success factors, your hobbies etc. It will be one central repository to showcase who you are?

You will be appreciated for providing ground details. If your client is confidential, perhaps you can mask the client name before sharing the link with the potential interviwers. Do ensure you share the details only with qualified propects, meaning the right recruiter for a large corporates. Otherwise, your template will be reused and available for all. Ensure your properietry information is maintained between you and the recruiter.

The following factors are evaluated by each of these departments to ensure the right candidate gets the job.

Candidate Selection Criteria

X – Indicates the status check.

SNo	Factors	TAG	Dept.	Mgmt	HR
1	Resume fitting the Job Description (JD)	X			
2	Technical Qualification		X		
3	Leadership Qualities, Team Management / Project Management			X	
4	Salary				X
5	Overall correctness of the resume				X
6	Background Verification				X
7	Resume format and error free	X			
8	Body Language, Psychology Test				X
9	Functional & Business Process Knowledge		X		
10	Preliminary Technical Round	X			
11	Face to Face discussions			X	

In most of the Organizations, recruitment process is a workflow enabled process, where in a candidate profile details are uploaded in a portal against a job reference number. Once a candidate passess through the first few rounds, the detailed score card is uploaded in the portal. After collating all necessary documents about the candidate and the interview test results, final assessment will be made by the respective HR team to ensure the right candidate will be hired for the job.

Often the process is not very transparent. It depends on the Orgnazation, as it takes anywhere between 5 days to 30 days for the entire interview process depending on the position, and panel's availability. As soon as a candidate clears the HR interview, HR team will finalize the salary as part of the negotiation phase. You will have a chance to negotiate, but you got to be careful not to lose the opportunity by being over ambitious.

You have to strike the right chord by doing your homework to identify the right salary for your skill, and experience and demand as per the market rate. Do not trust your neighbor's who often overstate the salary for societal peer pressure. You can check in the glassdor or any reliable portal to identify the market trend and the salary for your skills. Also, you can read blogs, reviews about an Organization in glassdoor.com.

Often times, interviewer will test to find the fitment in the job being offered and your willingness to work hard to proove you are the fittest of all other probable candidates. If you'd like to impress in a job interview..here are the few DO's and DON'T's that you should follow:

Do's:

1. Arrive on-time at the venue. At least 15 mins earlier and report to your interview coordinatore upon arrival.
2. Maintain eye contact with your recruiter.
3. Know the job nature, Organization through web site or through your friends.
4. Personal grooming is required. Dress for the occasion.
5. Your body language is important. Speak clearly and present yourself with confidence.
6. Do not undersell yourself. You have the right skill and you have every right to demand and deserve the best.
7. Carry a water bottle, snacks to avoid dehydration. Anticipate a longer wait time in jobfairs.
8. Take a few deep breaths to avoid getting stressed out.
9. If possible, get to know who is the interviewer. His role & responsibilities in the Organization.
10. Observe the surroundings..

11. Stay focussed throughout the interview and listen carefully to the questions and answer.
12. If you don't know..say "You don't Know" and do not try to fit in the right answer
13. If necessary go to the board and describe the process depending on the questions.
14. If you aren't clear, Do not assume. Instead, ask your interviewer to repeat it again. But do not do it very often.
15. You should justify yourself on how you would qualify for the job role
16. Go with a positive frame of mind
17. Be prepared to explain your career plan…2-3 years where do you envisage yourself such as developing into a Functional leader or a Project Manager etc.
18. If you'r on a telephonic, skype interview, ensure your microphone, picture quality is clear and do a test run with your friend prior to the actual interview
19. Do your research about the company, salary standards for the position applied for and the nature of the interview process to be well prepared
20. Maintain professionalism in the dress-code, behavior and smile as much as you can to make the discussions easy.
21. If asked, you may state your streangh's & weaknesses honestly based on your assessment.

22. A corporate might need your skill, as much as you need it. It is mutual, hence be confident that you're the best candidate for the job.
23. An interview rehearsal might help prior to the actual interview.
24. Ensure your scheduled date and venue. Try to visit a day before to avoid any surprises.
25. If you have several years of experience, state your strengths and drive a discussion around the technical, functional areas that you are very confident.
26. Be a good listener and then answer questions.
27. Your profile walkthrough should match with what you've done. You may articulate your profile succintly without reading it line by line. Start off with your accomplishments, projects and challenges.
28. Assess interview location, roadmap, bus route or car park, traffic etc.
29. Ask questions about your role, current team size, job nature and the project.
30. Demonstrate your strengths and indicate your willingness to improve on your weakness.
31. Maintain a positive demanor throughout the discussions and avoid side talks or phone.

32. Learn from your past mistakes and do not repeat.
33. Ensure you don't have any NDA signed before divulging your client details/projects in your profile.
34. What you speak should match with the profile like team size...challenges etc. You should be able to walkthrough your profile and focus on specific areas that would interest the interviewer.
35. Mentally be prepared to answer these questions:
    a. Tell me about yourself (2-3 mins)
    b. What do you know about this company...(2 mins)
    c. How do you fit into this role.
    d. Can you give me hard copy of your updated resume...
    e. What is your current CTC and what is your expectations. Are you open for negotiations?
    f. Explain this project to me...
    g. Tell me about your family.
    h. Are you willing to relocate?
    i. What is the role that you're looking for?
    j. Why do you want to move out of the current Organization?

Dont's:

1. Do not apply for a job without reviewing the job description and your fitment to the role.
2. Don't sound desperate as much as you need the job, The corporate will also need a good candidate like you.
3. Arriving late indicates lack of interest
4. A firm handshake will boost your confidence. The interviewer is another senior person who is calibrating your skills and overall fitment & by no means he is superiror to you. All are equal and someone might be just ahead in the professional career.
5. A poor format resume or with spell mistakes gets rejected in the first phase
6. Don't try to force yourself in fitting in to a job. If you find the position is not a viable option due to the lack of skill, be prepared to accept it and move on. Don't confront with the interviwer to proove yourself that you're the best. It is not the end of the World.
7. Do no ask questions about the client as it is confidential for any consulting organization. You may ask questions about the project & your roles.
8. First impression is your resume, hence be careful to walk through your resume starting from the academics till date with the dates memorized. It gives a negative impression, if an interviewer asks about

a specific project in your profile and if you are not clear.

9. Speak about the projects that would interest the interviewer based on the Job description and fitment.

10. Do not try to oversell yourself

11. Do not ask for compensation in a technical round or to a TAG associate in the first ground. It gives a bad impression as it is confidential to be discussed with the respective HR. In recent times, even technical Managers are asking this question, hence be prepared to address it carefully stating your expectations as it becomes a crucial factor in success of your interview.

12. Be prepared to give justifications to any breaks in-between jobs and most likely authentic reasons that can be justified with the documentary evidence.

13. Do not talk about the political issues you may had with your past employer. It will give a bad impression as though you're political.

14. Don't overstate about the projects, technology that you've used. It is easy to find out through the linkedin network.

15. If you go through the recruitment firms, instruct them what type of job they should apply for you. Do not allow them to send a mass mailer for jobs that you may not find it. It will embarrass the Organization and yourself.

16. There are some companies that may record the transcripts during the interview process. Hence, do not overstate or malign information to get into a job. Instead, you may speak honestly based on the real time experiences.

17. If you have a decade full of experience, you may cut short your discussions based on the job description and what is releant for the role applied for.

18. Do not ask for an onsite opportunity if the position applied for is offshore. It may lead the interviewer to believe that you're planning for an onsite role.

19. Do not indicate that you're willing to relocate if you don't have real plans to relocate. Instead you can state that you're willing to relocate based on the challenging opportunities presented.

20. Try to answer questions succintly and ask if the interviwer is fine with your response. If not, try to respond cleary with examples.

21. Apologize when necessary and never over do it. It shows your attitude.

22. Don't confront your interviewer. If you disagree, politely do so without much arguments.

There is no need to react to failures emotionally as you can achieve success through planning your career diligently. A word of caution to avoid conflict with the interviewing managers. You should understand their background to speak with functional or technical based on the interviewer's interest. If you use too many technology jargons to a PROJECT Head, may repel. You should be able to relate with simple terminolgy without much of acronyms. It's best to know your audience before you get deeper into the discussions.

If you get too many offers, ensure you take the right decision and inform the rest amicably without keeping them in the limbo. It would be unprofessional to keep somone waiting in the queue, especially an Organization. You should act professionaly to ensure the basic integrity is maintained during the interview process. If you do have 2-3 offers, ensure you keep one and reject the remaining offers.

Job Interview Process

E very candidate will go through the followings steps:

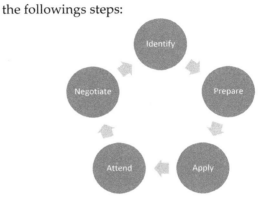

- **Identify:** You must read through the job role description atleast 5 times to understand the requirement. Try to parepare a simple list of what they are looking out for:
  - **Technical,**
  - **Functional,**
  - **Project Management,**
  - **Business Analyst**

And the domain expertise, technology etc. You may have this experience in this particular domain, however you can polish your resume to highlight these experiences. It is your responsibility to justify the interviwer that your profile matches the expertise.

- **Prepare:** You should prepare your profile diligently by highlighting the relevant experiences without overstating it. You should be careful as you should be able to articulate every singe point indicated in the profile. Hence, spending time in preparing your profile and rehearsal is essential.
- **Apply:** Apply directly through the right resources. The objective is to land your profile to the hiring manager. If you're going through an agency, ensure you discuss with them prior to sending the profile.
- **Attend:** Be confident while you attend the interview and ensure you speak out what is there in the profile.
- **Negotiate:** Finally, negotiate your benefits by assessing your skills with the Industry standards.

Your background should tell them a story, instead of too many detour in your career. In case of any breaks, be mentally prepared to justify as you might have had a sabattical due to a family situation. You may also explain the community services that you're engaged in which would add weightage to your profile. You should portray yourself as an active learner, listener and a leader thorugh continuous learning and empowerment. You may take up online courses, degree or PMI type of certifications to ensure staying ahead of the job market. Also, it is essential to build specialization around the domain expertise such as Automotive and within that you should master atleast one or more process areas such as "OTC – Order to Cash" cycle.

Often times during the interview process, there might be more than one interviwer, you must call out by names and answer their queries one by one. Do not rush through your answers. In most of the telephonic interviwers, there will be a panel of technical, functional and project managers interviewing you. You should listen carefully and respond to their questions and it is prudent to ask: *"Did I answer your question"*...Do not stray way beyond the specific response required. If you don't know, it's better to say so and move on to the next question. You should portray absolute professionalism during the interview process and demonstrate integrity as you're representing your years of experience. Even if you fail in an interview, people should consider you as a professional.

In some Geography such as Middle East, they address with Mr. or Ms. In Japan, they address you as "ABC" Sahn. You must be aware of cultural differences to suceed in a work environment. This would help you suceed in the work place. In Germany, where mostly are German speaking or in France, it is difficult to communicate in English. You should speak slowly and do not use too many jargons. Keep your communication simple and consice to help yourself connecting to the rest of the team. It is good to be passionate about a new job or the job that you're doing, but do not be emotionally attached with any job. Attend every interview as though it is your last chance and if you're in a job take one day at a time and perform to your best ability with integrity.

You should have the core principles at work to ensure you follow them throughout your career. Be a good listener, teacher to gain respect from your colleagues. In my view, it is a sheer waste of time to gossip negatively about someone and it would backfire you and too much of unwanted information that you pass to your colleauges would boomerang at you at some point. You should remember this...

'What you sow what you will reap up'

Instead, invest your quality time in spending time with your family, community service or technlogy blog or part time higher education or a certificate course. You profile should speak up your qualities. Also, do remember after 5 years of career, the job market would expect you to have lead projects, One of the qualities of leadership is to giving it back to the society or teaching. If you've done any of these, portray it during the interview session to establish your credibility. Technology is one aspect and people management, leadership is the other.

You should be able to comprehensively win the hearts of the interviewer. There may be some expections due to the quality of the interviewer. In most cases, they are trained to identifying the right talent and nurture them. If he/she is a good interviwer, then they will look at the good qualities in you, rather than asking questions such as 'what is the xxxxx' It may be needed to test your basic knowledge in the subject, however not in entirety. You will be adjudged based on the interpersonal skills, ability to handle pressure in tough situations, with your right attitude and aptitude to win business.

These are prime qualities that you should emulate and most of the leaders such as:
'Stephen Covey-Seven Habits of Highly Effective People' have described the building effective habits combined with your spiritual values. If you're able to adapt to the work culture with passion and inner values, you will emerge as a great leader. On the contrary, if you're complaining about the environment after joining in or too much of gossip about colleagues negatively or management, being extremely political and causing harm to others in the name of corporate politics would poison your heart first as per the intrinsic *'LAW OF NATURE'*.

Hence, it is best to identify the right job that would match your skills as life is too short to be complaining. You should enjoy going to work everyday and come back home in the evening with a sense of satisfaction and gratitude for having the opportunity to excel on a given day.

In my view, more you teach others, more you'll learn. Always be open to teach and help each other. I am not saying you should divulge confidential information about your project, you can help with technology without giving out your specific details to avoid unecessary flow of information that is not required. You should remember you're at work and your job is to perform to your best ability and make it conducive for everyone around you. It should be a pleasant experience going to work every day. In some work places, where there is extreme favoritism,,be careful and avoid uncessary confrontations. It may not help anyone, if you feel betrayed, you should hone your skills and take it as experiences in your life and move on.

These events unfolding around you at work, home is all manifestations of the Divine Nature and there is a bigger picture that you should always remember. Your karmas have formed the web of community, spouse, children, society and work around you. It has already been woven by the laws of Nature and the karma's specific to you. Hence, don't ask "Why ME" everyone has to go through the situations of pain, despair based on the karmic influences. My point is to keep yourself composed, calm and contemplate on the right approach to get away from the events or solve a problem without hurting each other at work, or relationships. The irony is that you would not even remember your so called 'bad' colleague after you leave the Organization. Your life is just a temporary and in continuum as your Atma is going through the experiences to relieving it from the karmic influences. What is the point in worrying about it and accusing an individual who might have done something to you?

You must learn from the past experiences…If you're challenged by your bosses.. thank them for provoking you to think beyond and thank everyone who had confronted with you. It will help you to move to the next level. You should build the habit and attitude of transforming a particular event or situation which you may call it as 'Negative' in to the positive zone with your outlook.

You may recall what Robert Bruce had said:

"My success is based on 99 failures"

Neither Thomas Alva Edison, nor Edison succeded in the first attempt. Their failures had made them stronger and the strongest and they survived through the storm to reach the shores and success happened through their diligence and hard work, and continuous learning from the mistakes and move on!

Most of the renowned CEO's & leaders of the current Technology era have learnt based on the experiences:

1.   Microsoft CEO, Bill Gates

2.   Mahatma Gandhi
3.   Swami Vivekananda
4.   Maharishi Vethathiri

These leaders are visionary and able to achieve through constant hard work and passion. You should try to emulate these leaders with great qualities. If you read through the history of each of these leaders, you'll be amazed how they had groomed themselves in to leadership. For example. Mahatma couldn't speak a single word in South Africa in his first argument in a court as a barrister. Likewise it happened to Swami Vivekananda who was unable to speak initially on-board in a ship to deliver a speech about hinduism.

Indeed, Swami Vivekananda's speech had transformed millions of Americans based on his speech about Vedanta in the World Religious conference held in 'Chicago'. A historical moment was written when he started his speech calling out: 'Ladies & Gentlemen' . His speech had transformed millions of US citizens in adapting a harmonious ways of living. So did swami. Paramahamsa Yogananda. Swami intrinsic breathing exercises helped millions of Americans in adapting a stress free life and disease free body. There is a great leadership talent in India, which has the ability to transform the World from time to time.

In the 12th Century, Boddhi Dharma had ventured into China to help millions of Chinese who suffered from diseases. He had learnt the skill of transforming pancha boothas, preparing medicines for chronic illness using herbs. It helped to save millions of chinese from an epidemic. He then taught villagers about the martial arts as a self defence to protect women and children.

Maharishi Vethathiri spoke about the World Peace in UNO, he had no proper education, through his persistence and efforts he had learnt English and science due to his passion and compassion to help the society. He had formulated the transformational techniques of kaya kalpa and aligning philosophy to Einstein's theory. His research thesis is being reviewed for the Noble price for the World Peace.

Your inner strength should compliment the outer to succeed. You have to be focused with core principles aligned with the laws Of Nature. You should medidate as a every day endeavor to succeed in life to lead a good quality of life encompassing good physical, mental and spiritual values as part of your DNA.

I strongly suggest not to end up in relationships with anyone in the reporting chain in your department. This might cause a lot of emotional stress. You should keep your relationship outside workplace to avoid emotional distress. If it happens, then ensure to move yourself to another department or your fiance to avoid any confrontations with the top management.

You should build your contingency corpus funds to support your family during a job loss. A financial planning is essential as soon as you land-up in a job. It should meticulously planned based on your real good family advisors and not a financial planner. I burnt my fingers investing in stock market in the US, which didn't help me gain anything as you need to carefully assess the market condition to become a mature and long term investor. I would rather suggest safer mode of investments which provides liquidity. One of the mode of safest investments include:

1. Government Bonds
2. Bank Fixed Deposits
3. Provident Funds
4. LIC

I would rank Provident Funds as the best option, since it will yield compound interest at 8-8.5%/Annum with a lock-in for 7 years only and then you can withdraw. I would recommend atleast one policy from LIC, and it helps in cash cruch situations in the form of loan against the policy. There are other investments such as Bonds, Fixed Deposits which are safer with its own lock-in period. The best option is the PF. You can have one A/C each for your family members and it serves the children education and your corpus in the future. All mutual funds and stock investments are subjected to the market risks and you cannot liquidate it at times of need. In my view it is all crap in paper money, unless it helps me in times of need and survival.

Perhaps, If you have a lot of money, you can invest 10-20% in stocks and another 20-30% in mutual funds. If you're surviving based on your hard earner money, please refrain from investing in any MNC based insurance companies, Mutual Funds and Stock investments, unless you have enough data to proove this would yield more than the PF % returns. In the longer run PF would yield substanital benefits and you will see your money grow through the compound interest. You can do a simple math of 1 L investment in a PF and see how much it would yield in 5 years at 8.5% interest compounded annually and compare it with your mutual funds or stocks which are 'subjected to the market risks'. In my view, only the politicians and the richest make money is stock investments as know the trend before-hand. I hope you understand the point. It's political anywhere in the World. Only a few handful make money in stocks. If you're an emotional investor, you will be taken for a ride.

It should be sustainable enough to take care of household expenses for atleast six months. As much as your grow higher in the career, a job chage will be difficult due to your children education, own house etc. You must evaluate pro's and con's of a job change and take necessary step only if it proves to be helpful in the longer run, say atleast 5 years from now. You must be aware of a short term gain will lead to losses and make yourself more marketable by analyzing the market trend, Industry, Economy and the political changes in the Government to take a right step ahead.   ***

Building A Winning Profile

Your profile speaks volume of sonnets.

Hence, it should be succintly describing projects, organization, team size and duration. Keep it simple and succint describing your role and responsibilities. A simple rule is that what you speak in the interview should match with the profile described.

A sample profile is indicated below for reference:

Name	First Name
	Last Name
Phone	+91 xxx xxx xxxx

Executive Summary	ABC is an IT professional with total X+ Years of IT experience, out of which X+ years of Project Management expertise. (3-4 sentences)

Key Accomplishments	▪ Achieved 30% realization benefits (TOP 5)

EXPERIENCE SUMMARY

YEAR	Organization	Roles	Responsibilities
Current			
Past I			
2			
3			
4			
5			

ACADEMIC BACKGROUND

Year	Education	Institute / University
1	Graduation	
2	HSC	

3	SSLC	

AWARDS/RECOGNITIONS

Year	Awards / Recognition	Organization

PROJECT DETAILS

ABC Technologies India Pvt Ltd
Apr 2, 2014 – June7, 2014

Project	-State your project here-		
Industry	Industry	Duration	From – To (MM/YY)
Client	-Name of the Client-	Employer	-Your Consulting Organization-
Role	-Your Role-	Team Size	-Overall Team Size-
Description	-Describe your project- (3-4 sentences)		
Responsibilities	-state your contribution towards the success of the project-		
Challenges	-What the key challenges that you faced-		
Achievement	-What are the significant achievements-		
Landscape	-Applicable for IT Leads/PMO-		
Functional	-Applicable for Functional, PMO's, Business process-		
Tools	-Applicable for IT Leads & PMO-		
Methodology	-Describe project management methodology-		

Contract Value	-Applicable for PM / Sales profile -
Bid Clientele details-	-Applicable for Bid Managers-
Project Type	

I would recommend maintaing an online profile, linkedin up-to-date and current and build your social professional network. You can blog, add content in youtube with your technology background to build a compelling profile in the social media space, as most of these companies are fishing out in the social media.

You can build your online, audio profile, webcasts to showcase your experience. You can create podcasts of your past projects as and when you complete a project to record and store it in your cloud space. If you are looking out for a job, perhaps it is easy to showcase your credentials with a one page profile summary guiding the recruiter to your cloud space with links of your video content, project podcasts to demonstrate your skill. However, you must ensure the job description fits in your profile. You must never quit jobs to seek out, as the market is very skeptical about the job seekers who are out of jobs.

Often TAG teams prefer employing someone who is on the notice period, and not someone who is on the ground without a project. If you're contemplating a job change, ensure you enable your naukri, monster or headhoncho profile online and check the opportunities. A job interview must be taken only if you're prepared and the basic hygiene indicated above is maintained. Otherwise you will be a curious seeker, without being an actual seeker.

It is easy to change jobs through your extended and professional network, rather than going through the job portals and/or through the recruitment firms. It is important to fine tune your profile that would interest your clients, however it doesn't indicate inflating your profile, instead seek out ways to gain confidence in your profile by highlighting what is important for a specific Organization that you are trying to get in. For example..a banking corp may be interested in your banking experience and other experience could remain in the back drop, whilst the mainstream profile should indicate your strengths, domain expertise and skills developed in the banking domain area of expertise.

If you have too many breaks, short term employment changes, it may hamper your chances of getting into large corporates as they identify your traits. You may be viewed as someone changing jobs too often. Hence, it is prudent to stay longer in an Organization and grow with them, instead of switching jobs in every summer. It is neither good for your career, nor for the Organization. Hence, I recommend staying longer in any organization, unless there are circumstances and strong reasons to move out. Always, plan for a 5 year term which would help you like a long term investor reaping up the benefits. If you're a short term investor, you'll have to incur losses such as loss of gratuity payments and opportunities to grow with the Organization.

You may have had a chance to move up in your career. If you swich too often, you would eventually lose 6 months – 1 year in the process of transition, which would delay your career progression. You must be diligent enough to understand your specific areas of interests, domain expertise and specialization. Once you narrow down your career path, stay invested..I mean stay through achieving your goals. Otherwise, if you're chasing money, then your career will become a zig-zag as a short-term investor. Perhaps you made money but only for a short term. Hence, you ask your employer regarding the career path after 5 years of onsite consulting role and what will be the path after that? Else you would ever remain as a consultant unless you decide to be…

You must socialize with the leadership teams to understand the Organization goals, review the competencies requiiired to align with the Organization goals to position yourself ahead of your peers through your continuous learning and opportunities to demonstrate your skills. Otherwise you will become like a 'cog in a wheel' as it happens in very larger Organizations as you will get stagnated without being able to achieve what you want.

Also, it is imperative to understand the Global initiatives, market trend and the overall segment strategies and growth. For example. we talk about

ERP, Analytics, E-Commerce, Geo-Informatics, Bio-Informatics, Mobility in every part of the world. If you drill down further, you will find the underlying technology excelling in each of these technology areas aligned to the business functions such as:

1. **ERP** – SAP, ORCL emerged as market leaders for domain - Manufacturing, Energy & Utilities, Logistics, Healthcare & Life Sciences.
2. **CRM** – SAP, SIEBEL (ORCL) emerged as market leaders for all domains
3. **HCM** – SAP, PeopleSoft (ORCL) emerged as market leaders
4. **SCM** – SAP, Kanban, ORCL
5. **ANALYTICS** – SAP BI/BO, ORCL DW, IBM BigData/Hadoop
6. **MOBILITY -** SAP Afaria platform for Mobile App. Development, JAVA/JSP for android and windows app development.
7. **Industry specific Solution: SAP IS- Oil & Gas, Utility & SAP IS-Auto**

Today, there is a lot of potential to become an entrepreneur. There is no right time to do it, you just need passion to start your own enterprise. For example. the success stories of flipcart, bookmyshow.com, bigbasket.com online e-commerce & retailing space indicate the fifth generation entrepreneurs who are smarter with least capital expenditure with long term vision. The next generation mobile app will run the enterprise, e-commerce as the internet era has metamorphosized into a mobility era.

The Mobility entrepreneurs will rule the next wave of enterprenership and it will happen in India and China as we have the largest consumer base in the Industry. If you are on a pursuit of a dream of becoming an entrepreneur...India is the place as we have the right talent with good infrastructure, we can go places rather than just being a services oriented Organization. The enterprise cloud is changing the IT landscape of our clients. Gone are the days with large IT infrastucture requirements, you can build your cloud based enterprise in days with critical business functions available as consumable services. You're ready to go in few weeks instead of months or years.

Career Progression

Your career progression depends on your interests, skills and what you like doing and doing your best in what you're doing.

By definition '*Career progression* refers to the upward movement or advancement made by ... Which level of *career progression* has substantial technical responsibilities?'. A simple pyramd highlights your progression mapping:

Competency Pyramid

The following competency pyramid will help you in acquiring the right technical, functional, business process knowledge and project management related skills to succeed in your progression.

Indeed, none becomes a leader overnight. It is a journey in your career path and the progression follows standard competencies to build. A leadership position will need strong functional, technical and the business process skills to succeed as a great leader. In order to build these skills it takes time and patience. If you're in the intial stages of a career, plan for acquiring good experience working in the technical / functional competency skill. Then, after few years in the Industry, you will be able to understand the core business process and the client requirements.

Once you're able to map client requirements to the IT environment, you have emerged as a project manager, who understand the requiremetns and be able to support delivery by leveraging the IT enablers. These enablers might be any technology that you've developed during the intial phase of your career. My point is to leverage your background experience as much as possible to build a solid career in a specific Industry verticals.

Once you align your background academics, tool skills and technology into one group of technical, functional and business process, it is easy to emerge as a leader in the domain. In additional to these skills, you will need to gain good people management skills. Your team should be able to acknowledge you as a leader who can mentor the team in times of need, and someone look upto emulate characters.

Often in large MNC Organizations, there is a strong emphasis in developing core competencies, people management skills, client facing, managing scope and expectations. In addition to these characteristics, managers / leaders are expected to lead from the front with strong integrity. Your background artifacts of the projects, people management, skills should emualte these characteristics to be able to succeed in a work place.

If you are building your career, cognizant of the fact developing your core competencies, aligned to the Industry would help you succeed. There is a lot of opportunites in the market right now. It depends on your passion and nature on what you would like to do and what you are best at. Here is a simple competency mapping of an IT Project Manager that you can explore:

Role	IT Project Manager
Core Skills	ERP, Mobility, BigData (Analytics)
Database	ORCL, SAP
Geography	EMEA, NA, APJ
Business Process	
Programming Languages	ABAP, PL/SQL, JAVA/JSP, .NET, Mobility
Domain Knowledge	Manufacturing
People Management	Handled large teams of > 50
HW	IBM 3090
Tools/Accelerators	ERP Tools
Certifications	PMP, SAP, ORCL, MSFT
Design Tools	ERWIN, mpp tool

You should plan your career early to acquire necessary skills. On an average in India the following statistics showcase our talent pool in MNC Organizations:

- 1-3 Years – Demonstrate your aptitude for learning new skills as Functional or Technical with hands-on skills development.
- >3-5 Years – Demonstrate your ability in Design, Develop applications in your core competency.
- >5-8 Years – Demonstrate leadership as a Team/Project Lead in the core competency and domain.
- > 8-10 Years – Demonstrate leadership in core and extended competencies in technical, functional and domain area of expertise as a Project Lead.
- > 10-12 Years – Demonstrate leadership in technical, functional and domain areas to execute projects with a large team size as a Project Manager
- > 12-15 Years – Demonstrate leadership in executing large projects with budgetary responsibilities as a Project Manager
- > 15-18 Years – Demonstrate leadership in executing large programs with a significant impact to the Organization as a Program Manager.
- > 18-20 Years – Demonstreate leadership with P&L responsibilities as a Head
- > 20-25 Years – Demonstreate leadership with handling multiple Accounts with P&L responsibilities as a Head or CTO/CFO type of executive roles.

There are Organizations hiring executives from premier MBA institues such as IAM's, IIT's; The above pyramid is a generic pattern of competency building in most of the MNC Organization.

If you are at the onsite location working as a Consultant without realizing the corporate dynamics, it will be difficult to align within the Organization. For example. A typical MNC corporate is aligned as follows as functional or competency based. The recent survey indicates a functional alignment in most of the service Organizations:

Industry Verticals	Manufacturing	Life Sciences	Automotive	Energy & Utility
Functions				
Supply Chain				
Procurement				
Finance				
HR				
Technology:				
IBM, SAP, ORCL, MSFT	X	X	X	

There is a lot of career options in any IT Organization as indicated below:

a) Hardware Engineer
b) Cloud Infrastructure Management
c) Network Engineer
d) OS Engineer
e) DBA (ORCL, BASIS-SAP, MSFT)
f) Software Developer (PL/SQL, ABAP, JAVA/JSP. Mobile Apps Developer)
g) Project Lead/Manager (Domain/Technology)
h) Functional Consultant / Manager (Domain)

i) Software Architect (Technology)
j) ERP Consultant (SAP, ORCL, MSFT)
k) Delivery Manager (Technology, Domain)
l) Program Manager (Process, Methods)
m) Practice Area Lead (Domain)
n) Mobile H/W Engineer (Java/JSP, SAP)
o) Mobile Apps. Developer
p) SW/HW Pre Sale Consultant (IBM. HP,)
q) SW/HW Sales Engineer / Consultant
r) Engagement Manager
s) Analytics (DW, BigData)
t) CRM, HCM, SCM, ERP Technical/Functional Consultant
u) Business Analyst
v) Freelancer in the domain areas of expertise
w) Business Consultant
x) Project Administrator
y) Project Coordinator
z) Finance Analyst
aa) Recruitment Lead

Types of Organization

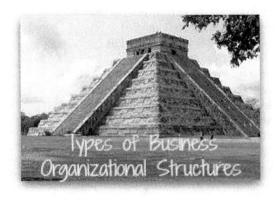

Large or small, every organization should operate with a defined organizational structure. A well thought out and strategic business configuration clarifies reporting relationships and supports good communication – resulting in efficient and effective work process flow.

The board and senior leadership should be the group who determines the type of organizational structure that would best support the internal operations, how work is carried out and the chain-of-command. There are different types of Organization…some of these are highlighted below with dynamics:

- MNC Matrix IT Consulting Services (IBM, Fujitsu, Accenture, Cap Gemini)
  - Global Consulting Services
  - Functional Organization

- Product Company (SAP, ORCL, MSFT, Talisma)
  - R&D
- Marketing Agencies
  - Sales & Marketing

What are the functional groupings of work processes?

Are there natural groupings of teams, work groups or units? Senior leadership looks at all functions and determines how they would like work activities to be organized and carried out. This process also identifies natural reporting relationships and chain-of-command. Reporting relationships can be both vertical as well as horizontal.

5 Common Business Organizational Structures

Matrix Organizational Structure

Example Matrix Organizational Chart

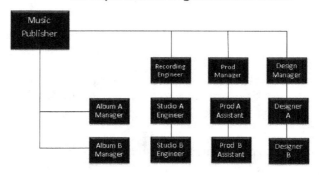

A matrix structure provides for reporting levels both horizontally as well as vertically. Employees may be part of a functional group (i.e. engineer) but may serve on a team that supports new product development (i.e. new album). This kind of structure may have members of different groups working together to develop a new product line. For example, a recording engineer who works for a music publisher, may have engineers who report to him but may also use his expertise and work with teams to develop new music albums.

The advantage of a matrix organizational structure is that employees have responsibility not only for their department but for organizational projects. A challenge with this type of structure presents itself when employees are given direction from two different managers and they need to prioritize their work responsibilities.

2. **Functional Organizational Structure**

Functional organizational structures are the most
Example Functional Organizational Chart

common. A structure of this type groups individuals by specific functions performed. Common departments such as human resources, accounting and purchasing are organized by separating each of these areas and managing them independently of the others.

For example, managers of different functional areas all report up to one director or vice president who has responsibility for all of the operational areas. The advantage of this type of structure is that functions are separated by expertise but the challenges comes in when different functional areas turn into silos that focus only on their area of responsibility and don't support the function of other departments.

3. Product Organizational Structure

Example Product Organizational Chart

Another common structure is to be organized by a specific product type. Each product group falls within the reporting structure of an executive and that person oversees everything related to that particular product line. For example an executive over Kraft products would be responsible for every product under that label – dressings, meats, sauces, etc. The advantage of this type of structure is that it organizes products by category but can create completely separate processes from other product lines within the organization.

4.Customer Organizational Structure

Example Customer Organizational Chart

There are many customer centric Organizations. They are organized by customer type. This is done in an effort to ensure specific customer expectations are met by a customized service approach. An example of this would be in healthcare. A patient seen as an outpatient has very different needs than those of patients who spend time in the hospital as inpatients. A customer centered structure creates customized care for those patients. The advantage of this type of structure is that it specializes in the needs of each customer group but can ignore the needs of different customer types.

5. Geographic Organizational Structure

Example Geographic Organizational Chart

Most of the MNC corporate are grouped by the respective geographic regions. This is done to better support logistical demands and differences in geographic customer needs.

Typically a structure that is organized by geographical regions reports up to a central oversight person. You see this type of structure in companies that go beyond a city or state limit and may have customers all across the country or in multiple states.

It is important to deliberate time and thought to design of an organization's structure. This is important to enable employees have a visual of how the organization functions and understands the chain-of-command. Operating within a defined structure, with good communication processes and work-flows, help to ensure efficient management of resources – people, time and money.

The work culture depends on the type of an Organization. If you choose an MNC Consulting services, you may have to be flexible to support clients in the US, EMEA as per their timings. In any product company, the product team will be responsible for development and the implementation team will be responsible for configuration of the product to a specific customer.

Most of the service based Organizations are aligned with the horizontal IT technology competencies aligned to the verticals as indicated below:

Manufacturing	LifeSciences	Logistics	Healthcare	Public Sector		

Functions: Business & Management, IT Consulting, PMO							
ERP							
SAP	ORCL	MSFT	CRM	HCM			
Mobility							

The respective competencies support the verticals across and the vertical teams will be responsible for managing the project. They will own the project with the support of horizontal competency implementing a project. The proceses, tools & methods are aligned as per the Industry standards. The respective vertical will provide required domain expertise during the scoping study to understand the client requriements. If you know the bigger picture, such as Organizational strategy, you will be able to grow within an Organization. Often manager's are responsible to cascading information from the leadership to the respective teams reporting to them. The HR functions are align with the corporate initiatives. It is your responsibility to undrestand the operating procedures, year end appraisal process and the performance review process. Otherwise, you will be suprirsed to hear it out loud from your manager by the end of the year.

When you start on a project, ensure you understand the basic hygiene to be able to successfully translate skills to tangible output. Unless you're viewed as highly productive resource by the management, you'll not grow, keeping the human politics aside. It is natural to think different and confrontations are part of the Organizational culture. Hence, do not brag about these issues. If it goes beyond a certain limit, call it out and move on with in the Organization or perhaps outside the Organization. There is no point in losing your heart for trivial reasons. Keep your expections loud and clear in terms of maintaing physical, mental and spiritual growth. Ensure your Organization takes care of your basic birth right of these aspects, If not they are using you as a commodity, Perhaps, you should seek justice. If you're unable to get justice, then call it out. Sky is the limit and World is your home, where you can work anywhere. In my view, if any Organization does not allow you to be yourself, watch out you're being commoditized. Hence, check out the characteristics of Organization:

1. Transparent,
2. Honest,
3. Ethical,
4. Value Clientele relationships,
5. Care for the Employees (Human Values) &
6. Flexibility & Integrity.

We are not in Germany under Adolf Hitler. If any Organization is treating you like a commodity, then you should think about moving ahead in your career by upscaling your skills, instead of taking up negative vibes, which is not good for your health. Hence, you should be aware of your surroundings, company's corporate policies and retrenchment. If your company let you go for the market reasons, don't lose your heart. You have the entire World to explore. If your technology has wane down, there is always scope for mastering another technology. After all it will take 3-6 months duration to building expertise in any field of interests based on your diligence.

My recommendation is to build enough contingency for taking care of monthly expenses. This corpus fund would help you in case you are jobless and you don't need to worry for atleast six months. It would help you to stay focussed and pursue your dream career. You will need to spot out subtle messages from the management team in case the company is not doing good & there is a possibility of retrenchment..or perhaps you're being asked to relocate. Be open and discuss with your manager. It is imperative to sort things out before it gets out of your hands, which would surprise you.

If you'r using skype for the interview process, ensure your mobile camera is of good quality and sound is good. I would typically do a couple of rounds of trial interview, prior to the actual one to avoid frustrations. Ensure your resume is updated atleast once in every six months and build a portal detailing your projects, in case of confidentiality mask the client name and build a comprehensive case study, podcast. These are valuables that you can discuss in a real interview.

Ensure you're prepared end of every year with an updated profile, active with a portal links walking through your profile, with every bit of specifics such as the clientele Geography, exact date of start and end, duration of the project, team size and share the success stories, challenges in podcast. You must do this for atleasat major projects that you've executed. If your projects have failed, ensure you capture the artifacts of the failure and reasons for it. It will guide the interviewer to think about your due diligence and attentiveness to the greater details.

You must consolidate feedback and ensure you include a feedback link to the portal to ensure these artifacts are captured. Your certificates, awards and manager's feedback are all valuable information that you can add to the portal. It will be a repository to demonstrate to your interviewer or just to keep a consolidated view of your professional career. I believe 2-3 years from now, recruitment would be entirely through the social media. Utilize Linkedin, Facebook, Youtube to socialize your profile with a team of specialized resources with a video profile that explains about yourself. You must download necessary apps in to your mobile such as Naukri, glassdoor to keep an eye on the job market from time-to-time.

You may assess your interests based on your analytical skills and the job opportunities in the IT market. Once you gain a decade full of experience, you would be able to fit in most of the management positions with your ability to learn quickly across technologies. At some point you should move higher above the technology into functional and domain areas of expertise to grow in the P&L areas of expertise in managing large enterprise accounts.

It is always better to exhaust the opportunities in the current Organization. If you're not able to suceed in the endeavor, then seek out opportunities. Perhaps, we take decisions emotionally based on a confronting situation with your immediate manager. You may seek out to different groups, HR to identify a potential match as you have established network, legacy. It is imperative to seek opportunities within the current Organization to seize the opportunities as you've established a legacy and it takes less time to assimilate, when compared to a new organization.

Often times I have observed, those are working with large Organizations struggle initially to work with a small or mid sized Organizations due to the change in dynamics. A large Organization might have its own standards and procedures that may not be easily transferrable in the market place such as specific PMI, Project Methodology. You have to do some ground work in polishing your profile by highlighting the larger picture of the procedures in order to aligning with the Global processes. You have an advantage of expertise gained by working with a large corporate, now it is your responsibility to emphasize on the expertise that you will demonstrate in the newer Organization. You should be mentally prepared to go through petty politics, people and process related issues in any mid-sized or small Organizations.

Mostly in India, the small and mid-sized Organizations are run by a group of men and it is people oriented. In large MNC corporates it is based on policies and procedures. This may not be the case in small Organizations. Hence, You will need to know the Organizational dynamics by observing things around you, your peers and mentors. In India, people are expected to hit the ground running and there is no concept of mentorship to assimilate you in to the culture. Perhaps it may be warm or cold, be prepared to seek out to the respective managers assigned. You should build your network and talk to colleagues as first couple of months are crucial to succeed in any job. You should know which department you belong to and how you're aligned within your Organization, your department goals and your manager's KPI to align with the Organizational goals.

Do not hesitate to introduce yourself first and seek out friendship in establishing a good network during the initial cooling period. Once you settle down, ensure you discuss about your goals and objectives and set the expectations clear. If you don't know any subject, seek out assistance with any formal or informal training plan to gain required knowledge to do the job. In India, mostly you should seek out and ask questions, rather than awaiting for an angel guiding you through the process.

Managing Expectations

"In business, the competition will bite you if you keep running; if you stand still, they will swallow you."

You have to manage expectations whether you are working with your esteemed clients or dealing in relationships. By setting the right expectations, you can avoid a lot of frustrations. Indeed, this will apply to the job match as well. If you're clear in what you want, you can get what you deserve in the market. For example. If you have constraints in location, work schedule and pay etc. You will need to apply for the companies that offers you the conducive environment without impacting your personal life as you might be focusing on striking a work-life balance. As a job seeker, the following factors will need to reviewed to set the expectations right:

62

1. Your salary expectations in line with the Industry standards with % increment from the current employer.

2. Work location, culture and schedule as you may expect a flexible work-culture.

3. Does it require you to work in shifts based on the US or EUR operations?

4. Do you have plans to relocate to the onsite. What is your career aspirations? Is the job offered in line with your career aspirations.

5. Does the role defined and clear with job functions.? Does it interest you to proove.

6. Did you check for blogs about the company such as glassdoor on policies and how employees are treated

7. Did you survey about the potential employer for historical evidence of retrenchment during slow market conditions

8. Is this company solid in terms of balance sheets, investors and funds available.

9. Did you checkout from your linkenin type of professional network for company's rating and employee referrals?

10. Did you checkout the past performance of the company, product lines and the future strategy?

11. How long have they been in existence and what is the historical evidence of successful execution of projects in maintaing clientele relationships.

12. What is the management operating style? Is it flexible for innovation?

13. Do you get an opportunity to grow in the Organization. Did you get a chance to

interview anyone in the Organization to discuss the growth potential.

14. What is their contribution to the society?
15. Did you checkout the profile of the CEO in the US/EUR or local MD who is operating in India?
16. What is their operational excellence?
17. What are the benefits offered to the employees and what % variable is awarded on an average?
18. Are there too many long timers > 5 years staying with the Organization.

You will need to probe in to the Organization work culture, past performance and working dynamics, clientele relationships by connecting through your professional network, interviews to your peer's and colleagues network. This would help you assess an appropriate score of an Organization. It is essential to seek out 2-3 weeks of time before you join the Organization. There are paid surveys, glassdoor portal that will provide valuable insights about the Organization. You will need to conduct a detailed survey before you accept an offer.

I was shocked by one of the companies that offered me an onsite salary as an ERP professional. A local state based Organization in South India that had offered me lucrative salary, family benefits and relocation expenses at onsite in the Middle East. Apparently, after having accepted the offer, and resigned from the current employer…each of the status came to the plight one after the other. First one, they said I was offered a placement in their office in Qatar as a Delivery Manager-Qatar and then it was changed to Delivery Manager – KSA.

After even accepting the location change, I came to know that they were struggling to process 'IQAMA' a long term work permits in the Region. Hence, the chances of bringing in my family was nil. Second, they didn't pay even the basic salary for couple of months and third they said the onsite salary was no longer valid, hence I had to settle with the lower India based salary which was 30% lower than the earlier income, despite being at onsite-KSA as a Delivery Manager.

I went through a lot of mental stress and trauma after having rejected offers from top 5 consulting companies for having accepted this position with a local compnay for the onsite position. Unfortunately, my career went down the cross roads due to the unforseen affairs. This was beyond comprehension, and I had to rush back to India in an overnight flight from Dammam to evade the situation. It became an instance, which helped me to gain immense experience. Though my only take aways have been good projects and clientele that I was able to interact during my stint in the region. The bottom line of my story is to conduct a detailed survey about the company, checkout with someone in the similar role and if possible try to talk to the insider in a similar position and how he views the organization. If you are applying for a Project Manager and if you talk to a Developer, you may not get the right view. Hence, it is prudent to fish out the right information based on conducting surveys, interviews and insider information in the portal.

The following factors need to be considered before accepting a job offer:

1. Conducting Surveys,
2. Growth Opportunities,
3. Past History,
4. Sound Financials,

5.   Flexi work-culture,

6.   Good Clientele relationship

7.   Checkout if they have offices in the region operation. If it is in EUR, check if they have registered as per the operating procedures.

8.   Integrity of the Management

9.   Review the management profile of the company and fish out details of who they are by checking in the Linkedin profile.

The above factors are apparent with large and Global consulting Organizations, however with several small and mid-sized Organizations promising phenomenal growth..you will need to watch out for any signs of discomfort. Most importantly, you must review all documents prior to signing any agreement with the Organization. If you're asked to sign it during the induction program, ask for one day time to check with your legal references. Otherwise, you are in for all sorts of trouble from NDA's to the exit procedures. There are lot of small, and mid-sized Organizations take your weakness points as their strengths to lure you with false promises such as:

1.   Onsite Salary in USD $$$

2.   Long term assignments in Other Region

3.   Family visa sponsorship

4.   Using name of their partners in the Region.

Our human tendency is to get attraced by the onsite salary /annum, however you would never know if the duration of the project will last as promised and the company is stable. Though I love working in this region and my clientele, you cannot trust the small companies promising placements or projects in the MENA Region unless someone in that country could do a little bit of investigation on your behalf.

You have to be extra careful while venturing into the MENA Region as the operating model is different and there are no strict measures to help employees. Hence, you will need to conduct a detailed due diligence prior to accepting any offer. Once you're landed in that region, you're at their mercy. You may not get salary on-time, as promised or not even the salary that was promised to you at the time of offering you a job! These companies are shameless and lure you at any cost and they don't operate with integrity. There are plenty of miscellaneous challenges in the MENA region such as:

a) Visa constraints for self and family.
b) Payment cannot be credited into the bank account in KSA as you cannot create a bank account. Alliance with the local partner need to be verified Nature of contract, tenure and the payment mode will need to be verified upfront prior to accepting the offer

In any case, a detailed survey of the above parameters would help you assess the situation prior to accepting an offer. These companies operate with a modus operandi where in they lure intellectuals with fake salary and promises. A fresher can stake his career for less pay to gain experience at the expense of the family, but not for the professionals with immense experience, who cannot stake his/her career with these type of third-rate companies, as it would detour your career path. Upon your return you will not be able to get back to the Organizations in India as TAG teams would ask for specific justifications.

Typically, for a mid-career professionals it may take anywhere between 3-6 months to get back on the career track to land on a job of his/her preference, hence it is mandatory to build enough contingency funds to remain with required liquidity for atleast six months. These are the issues if you falter in any of the steps while trying to venture into a high risk region such as MENA. Infact, these companies lure you by saying non-taxable salary or large Oil Corp etc. etc. However, the reality might be different. You would lose your credibility at an onsite location, and you will become vulnerable in the region like MENA if you have not done your due diligence part.

Your career is not about risk taking apetite. It is a financial risk, and issues in terms of stability if you aren't planning it right. Hence you will need to be absolutely clear prior to taking steps in your career, cognizant about the fact of your long terms goals. Ofcourse money will follow if you prove your worthiness in any specific domain. I know a lot of my colleagues who have ventured into setting up their own BPI/KPO's have flourished. It is important to assess scope of the Industry, your risk taking apetite and capital investment.

If you have the background in the Industry, it would help you assess scope of risks and mitigation plan. Otherwise you would be a spectator watching your finances melting away. Hence, it is imperative to conduct a detailed study in any field wether a job change or your own enterprise setup, need to spend atleast six months to a year with market survey, interviews and the Industry trend, skills availability etc. If you're are entering into business opportunity without even venturing into these details, perhaps you're seeking trouble. You will never be able to gain lost money and time. You would be able to achieve success with a detailed project plan and task level plan by every day and discussing with peers in the Industry with immense experience.

One of the gentleman approached me to help me setup a BPO/KPO company, though I was initially fascinated by his clientele..I couldn't verify his legitamacy. Hence, I had to stop all my business startup plans. You will need to reach out through the right professional network and investigate prior to signing any agreement for partnerships plan or investing money trusting someone. You will not be be able to connect all loose ends in the end with another failing enterprise. Indeed, this gentleman even failed to explain me the ROI calculations and the monthly payment. Their modus operandi is very simple by luring your in USD $$ or UKI lbs. thereby overstating the benefits. In reality the SLA's in BPO/KPO has never beeen realistic, hence you will never achieve the 100% profitability as you may expect. Instead, work with a BPO/KPO to see for yourself before even venturing into it.

If you have real good ideas such as cloud enterprise, you may seek partners from your professional network and build a solid business plan, project plan and your goals. You will need to checkout if the real market exists for the products or services that you're trying to venture. You must have a long term vision to suceed in the market plance, and your apetite for risks, investments and ROI can take longer depending on the market with additional opex expenses in terms of salary payments, infrastructure and rentals etc. These factors play a predominant factor in determining your ability to work or become an entrepreneur. Ensure you take necessary steps prior to the venture. Never do anything in a state of hurry!!! Do not accept job offers in a week or perhaps a partnership agreement, however attractive it may be. Take you time, do enough research and then take a right call after all the research and evidence of success ahead. This approach would help you achieve success without much frustrations.

You have the right to ask appropriate questions during the interview process. It is always mutual. In India, our professionals are too humble and the job market is buoyant, hence we tend to shy away from asking questions. It is better to ask now, rather than repenting later as I did. You must contemplate on your career options by taking it to your heart as you may gather information from many sources, however it is your responsibility to call out the right decision.

I took a decision emotionally resulting in leaving an MNC to accept an offer at onsite-KSA (Saudi Arabia) through a very small Organization, which had become a bigger challenge to get out of the Organization to get back on-track. Hence, take decisions by heart when you're quiet. Taek a few deep breaths and contemplate on the job offers, partnership offers or investing your hard earned money or perhaps venturing in to foreign land by assessing pro's & con's to find out the best option that will suit you. End of the day it is your family and you who are going to gain or lose and none can help you in the predicament if you take a wrong decision.

Finally, a job change might pose enormous stress in terms of finances and the stability. You career is on the cross roads and you will need to start all over in prooving yourself. Be prepared for the worst and do not expect a dream company to arrive soon. You must be prepared for a delay in getting placements as it depends on the market, quarter of the year and your Industry performance on the whole.

Hence, you will need to survive with the contingency funds available and keep your expenses to the bare minimum to avoid any unpleasant surprises. You may not be in a position to accept a job offer in North East or West as you may have family constraints and other issues in immediate relocation. Perhaps, as an option you can accept the offer and keep trying. Often times, my observation is that TAG teams respect you when you're on the job. If you're out of the job and searching, you're at their mercy.

My strong recommendation to each of you is to try for a better job if need be, while you are on a job. Otherwise you will get desperate financiallly depending on the situation or perhaps the TAG teams may take you for granted by offering low pay and long waiting to hear post the interviews. Your skills are considered to be hot only while you're engaged, if you're out then you are considered to be incapable or perhaps you will need to take additional steps to explain the sabatical or the break in-between the job.

It is even prudent to take up training or enhancing your skills to broaden your scope of work to ensure you get jobs. Hence, read through the job sites, market trend to see what is hot in the market such as bigdata/hadoop or ERP and assess your background can be easily transferred to the upcoming opportunity. When you upscale yourself in the domain area of expertise, make sure your past history helps you in fetching a job. It should not look like you were desperately seeking jobs, hence the switch to a different technlogy. For someone in Mainframe can manouver with the IBM Mainframe technology such as COBOL, CICS, IMS, JCL's, DB2 which can help you transfer your skills to scope of work in that area, you can showcase your profile as enhancing, growing in the domain rather than blindly switching from Cobol to Mobility apps development.

You have to assess where you stand and where you want to be 5 years from now. How transferrable are you in the Industry and flexible. My perception about the market is that every 5 years the skills is worning out. Even ERP's such as SAP is a commodity now and mobility apps development, BigData will become commodity in 5 years from now. Hence, "you will need to make hay while the sun shines" Once the skills become little older, utilize this background to showcase domain area of expertise in BFSI, or Manufacturing to claim your leadership positions. You will need get certified in ITIL, PMP for managers and certifications for respective ERP areas to ensure you stay ahead of peers in the Industry.

You will need to reskill and re-certify yourself every 2-3 years to remain in the race course. Else, you will lose out the opportunities. If you are not in any financial constraints, then you have plenty of options to switch between industries as India is gaining momemtum in BFSI, Healthcare or even R&D and product development. I got a very lucrative offer from a small product development company for developing ERP for Higher Education. It sounded very exciting. If you are financially stable, perhaps you can take calculated risks. Otherwise stay around the core specialization areas where you are the master, where you have the monopoly!

Above all, I respect my work life balance. Though I enjoy work, working long hours at the expense of my health is not my cup of tea! You must be aware of strikiing a balance in relationships, work and balance it as two parallel tracks. You will need to spend time with your kids and challenges in the family to shape them, as it is your responsibility as a parent. The parental pressure is enormous..you will need to deal with that.

Five steps for managing client expectations:

1. **Be Honest From The Get-Go.** Though it may sound counterintuitive, I always tell potential new clients in the very first initial conversation about *possibly*working together that there are no guarantees. As with most things in life, there are too many factors at play to make any grandiose promises. I can't predict whether a producer will like a pitch, or a reporter will quote my client. Although it may feel uncomfortable, I think that saying this clearly and in no uncertain terms, positions the client to take a leap of faith in your work and also helps them to understand the process behind your work.

2. **Under-**Promise **, Over-Deliver.** This old adage is one to live by! I promise my clients that they will have immediate & constant access to me and my team; that we will, every day, work on their behalf through pitching and meetings with the media; and that if nothing else, it is guaranteed that they will become known to key members of the media. After that, when big interviews start rolling in, it's much more appreciated!

3. **Anticipate the Client's Needs Before** *They* **Know Their Own Need.** This one definitely takes time and practice, but think about it: no one knows your business as well as you do. You know when

things are going great and when you need to ramp up your efforts. It's so important to share that with a client through a simple email stating "I'm going to spend extra time this week working on your project – I really want to get you out there as much as you do." It can go a long way.

4. **Constant Communication**. If you're in the service industry of any kind, that is what you do – serve. That means being bubbly, bright and (almost) always available. While of course it's important to set boundaries so that you can maintain a rewarding personal life, it's critical that your clients know they can gain access to you as needed. Hopefully just knowing you're available and ready to jump on a project as needed will be enough so that your client's won't abuse your generousity with time.

5. **Reports**. Probably not anyone's favorite task during the week, but reports show a clear delineation of work that was done over the course of a week or month. Remember – reports don't have to be very long, or in a format that clogs up a lot of your time. A simple email detailing tasks completed for the week shows your clients what they're paying for, and thus, keeps them happy.

Hopefully, by following these steps, you'll be on a road to an even better relationship with your clients. By following this process, you'll most likely achieve better results in your work, too. You must be spiritually aligned, and logically inclined with pragmatic approach to suceed as a leader.

I wish you all good luck in your career ahead!!

Job Failure – A stepping stone for Success!

If you fail in any job interview or end up with a poor rating in a year end appraisal, do not lose heart. I firmly believe in learning from the failures and grow. It is a great opportunity provided by the Divine Nature to help you succeed.

It depends on lot of factors such as:

1. Your performance compared with others in the Dept.
2. Management review of your diversified skills
3. Your adaptability wthin the Organization

4. Interperosnnel and management skills
5. Technology expertise
6. Project / Clientel feedback
7. Your interests levels in the subject ..passion

Above all, the human touch which forms the basic reason for a poor rating. Beyond the algorithm that builds the rating rules, the human touch is the final call. In any department, manager is responsible for the ultimate rating based on the consolidated feedback from your supervisors If you've not performed as per the expected standards, there is always a scope for learning. There is no need to feel disappointed. In India, most of these decsions are also based on the cultural, political or personal touch and often not just the rules of algorithm. I hope the situation will change with large MNC's embarking the shores of India, the policies will change for helping each other.

In the future, all IT professionals should form groups, unions to support each other, to avoid Organizations treating you like commodities, by sharing your experiences and the issues that should become public. It is a mandate to support women working late by providing secured cab services or work from home options. If any Organization is violating these basic operating procedures, you must bring it to the public through appropriate media. You must be aware of the basic labor laws to understand your value. Again, remember you're skilled and rendering services to an Organization and you deserve respect.

We are equal, not biased based on the color, creed, religion..These geographies are one and the same and none should be treated like Royals..You have the same ability, capability like your manager and your manager and you are made of the same intelligence guiding us. Hence, understand your value and work mutually to benefit. Be open, honest and professional!!!

Instead of going through an emotional truama of layoff...gather strength and move on with your career. It is not the end of the World as often I hear people crying. Just accept it and move on. If you're a technocrat, align yourself with the right technolgy based on the study about the technology, investors, stock value and the market in next 5 years. I believe a typical cycle of a software product ranges between 10-15 years max. for a good product. Hence, you should be able to transfer or broaden you skills in to wide areas every 10 years by socializing with the leaders in the respective domain areas through technology blogs. If you're a manager, ensure you have the right certifications and the functional domain areas of expertise.

You will have a rewarding career ahead!!!!

Epilogue

In the end it depends on how you carry yourself during the interview. You must plan ahead in your career and how you want to visualize yourself 5 years from now and build relevant competencies in terms of technical, functional, domain and project maanagement capabilities. Once you gain required competencies you can present youreslf self and be prepared to answer all queries from the interviewer. Often times we lose focus and concentrate only on the job, it is required to study the subject as it will give you valuable insignts. If you're in to ERP consulting, there is a lot of scope of studying new topics almost every day.

Your self esteem, presentation skills and project management capability combined with the technical, functional and domain expertise will get you the job that you deserve. End of the day, it is not just the company looking for a good candidate, it is also a good candidate looking for a good company, Hence, ensure you do due diligence about the company, politics, culture etc. before you take the next step.

Once you have required details and the offer. You may negotiate the best offer to join the new company..

You must stay warm,
Stay hungry for knowledge,
To achieve the highest feat of success;

If you're a master,
In what you do,
You will deserve the best;

If you're clinical in
Your operations,
Your company will entrust you;

If you're humble,
You'll be rewarded;
If you're passionate and innovative,
You'll become a leader!!!

I wish you all the best !!!!

*

Nature!!!

She awaits your return to turn back home,
The eternal grace is ever waiting,
Like a breast of a mom,
Waiting to feed her child!

She is our universal mom,
She hates none,
And remains a pauper!

She is ever loving,
Caring in dissipating love!
To our dismay,
We mourn for mundane events
Without realizing the mother Nature!

She plays havoc when you need a jolt
To think, realize and get back to the roots!
Would anyone deny?

She is an eternal love,
Listening to you here and now!
Whereas you're miles away from her,
She waits at the door steps as sun shine
And returns back to you as a moon light!

She calls you by name
And loves you by heart!
Who cares for mom's love?
As I fall back, cry deeply,
She is there with open arms
Reminding of my childhood in her womb!
The Universal womb is awaiting your return!!!